J

DATE DUE

JUN 25 1984	1349	Ag 22 '90	02279
DEC 10 1984	783	No 26	04570
APR 15 1985	1142	JUN 27 1990	04059
JAN 23 1986	711	JUL. 1 7 1991	4059
NOV 8 1986	158	AUG. 1 9 1991	19413
DEC 7 1986	158	NOV. 1 1 1991	8670
JB 2 9 87	02279		
Ja 19 '88	1500		
Jl 20 '88	1142		
No 30 88	03781		
De 14 88	2871		
No 2 93	934		

The Little Kid's
FOUR SEASONS
Craft Book

Jackie Vermeer and
Marian Lariviere

The Little Kid's
FOUR SEASONS
Craft Book

Taplinger Publishing Company · New York

Also by Jackie Vermeer and Marian Lariviere
THE LITTLE KID'S CRAFT BOOK

First Edition

Published in the United States in 1974 by
TAPLINGER PUBLISHING CO., INC.
New York, New York

Published simultaneously in the Dominion of Canada by
Burns & MacEachern, Ltd., Toronto

Library of Congress Catalog Card Number: 73-18791

ISBN 0-8008-4926-4

Designed by The Etheredges

ACKNOWLEDGMENTS

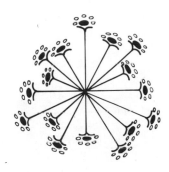

We thank our families and friends for their interest and support during this endeavor. We are grateful to the following people for loaning us many of the creative examples shown in this book: Robert E. Allen, Jennifer L. Bylund, Darlene Chapman, H. Richard Frew, Todd Lariviere, Neal Lariviere, Jane Rocke, Marna Schlegal, David Vermeer, and Kristin Vermeer. We also thank Paul McMaster for his excellent photographic work.

All color and black and white photography by Paul McMaster. All drawings and illustrations by the authors.

CONTENTS

ILLUSTRATIONS IN COLOR

The Little Kid's
FOUR SEASONS
Craft Book

A WORD ABOUT SUPPLIES

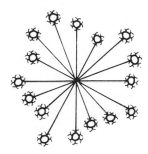

Choosing the proper supplies for children is important. A few of the basics for younger children are large crayons, blunt-nosed scissors, and wide brushes. Older children can more readily adapt to an increased variety of materials.

Water-base paints are best for children for cleanup reasons. Tempera paint can be purchased dry or mixed, and can be used in most any painting situation. Acrylic paints will work equally well—in some cases better—but are more expensive.

White glue is generally recommended as it is strong and dries clear. Paste will do, but it has a tendency to lose its holding strength after drying.

In addition to the usual kinds of paper (drawing, typing, construction, and newspaper) there are other possibilities to consider.

Working with dough

Old wallpaper, butcher paper, wrapping paper, the tissue and cardboards that come in folded clothing—any of these would add new interest to a project. In general, think before you throw something away, it may still be useful.

There are a number of projects throughout this book that are made from dough. To avoid repetition, the recipe is given here.

DOUGH RECIPE

4 cups flour	*1½ cups water*
1 cup salt	*Food coloring (optional)*

Mix together with your hands. If the dough is too sticky, add more flour. Knead for 4 to 6 minutes. Dough can be used immediately or stored in plastic wrap. Shape the desired figures, and place on a cake rack or aluminum-covered cookie sheet for baking. Bake small items at 350°F for 1 hour. Bake large or thick items at 250°F for 3 or more hours—until hard and golden brown.

The projects presented can be adapted to a wide range of abilities. Some projects will require more preparation for use with younger children, whereas older children will be able to complete them with a minimum of instruction. A few of the processes, such as the crayon batik, will require adult participation. Regardless of the child's age or ability, the basic objective throughout is to encourage his creative growth.

FALL

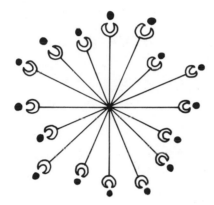

Fall is a season of changes—school begins, leaves turn color, and the holiday season approaches. These changes afford many opportunities for craft projects.

Taking your child on an autumn walk is a good way to show him the changes that occur in this season. It is also a great time to observe the many varieties of seedpods and leaves, and you may want to collect samples of the more interesting kinds.

One way to use some of the seedpods is to make a collage. For the background it is best to use cardboard, in order to support the weight of the pods. The child can arrange the pods to form his own design and glue them in place.

Seedpod collage

Autumn leaves and colored cardboard can be combined to form a lovely picture. The picture in the photograph uses different kinds of leaves and a "found" butterfly. When butterflies have completed their life cycle they die, and if found, make a delightful addition.

Making a nature collage

Leaf and butterfly picture

Leaf picture with twig frame

Children enjoy forming their pictures with the colorful leaves, which are then glued in place. Although the leaves may be brightly colored at first, the child should be prepared to have some of the color fade after a short time. A fitting frame for this kind of picture can be made from pieces of twigs.

A fallen branch with an odd shape may be intriguing to a child. Encourage him to add a portion of it to his collection. Some of these small branches can be attractively displayed in a dough vase. Make the dough according to the recipe on page 13. After the child has created his vase, and it has been baked, he can then arrange the branches. The vase can be painted with acrylic paints, if desired. This makes a nice gift for any nature lover.

Dried arrangement of eucalyptus leaves

Some of the larger individual leaves that were collected on the nature walk can be used in creating an unusual picture like the one shown in color opposite page 32.

Begin by placing several of these leaves on a large piece of construction paper and tracing around the edges. To add color, dip pieces of sponge into tempera paint and apply to the leaf area. It is best to provide small pieces of sponge, as these are easier for the child to handle. A selection of fall colors gives the child the opportunity to paint his leaves as he wishes. Each color should be put in a small shallow container, for ease in dipping. When the paint has dried, a construction-paper frame can be added.

A way to preserve some of the more interesting leaves and weeds is to press them between sheets of waxed paper. The natural material should still be in a soft stage, not crisp, as it will break and come apart. Place the leaves or weeds on a sheet of waxed paper. Additional color is added by sprinkling the surrounding areas with grated crayon. Cover with a second sheet of waxed paper and press with a warm iron. The pressing should be done on several layers of newspaper, to absorb the excess wax. Children like to do the pressing because they enjoy watching the colors melt and blend. To bring out the colors, place the picture on a piece of white construction paper, add a frame, and staple together. A group of these unframed make delightful placemats.

When your child becomes aware of differences in leaf shapes, it is a good time to encourage his interest by having him start a leaf collection. Let him choose some of his favorite leaves to glue onto pieces of cardboard. Each leaf should be identified and the name

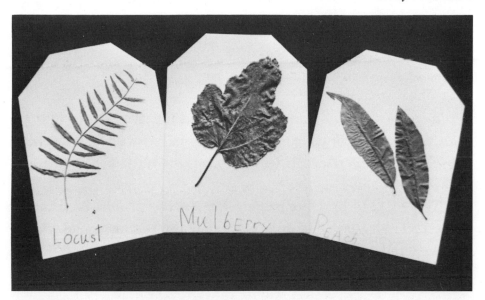

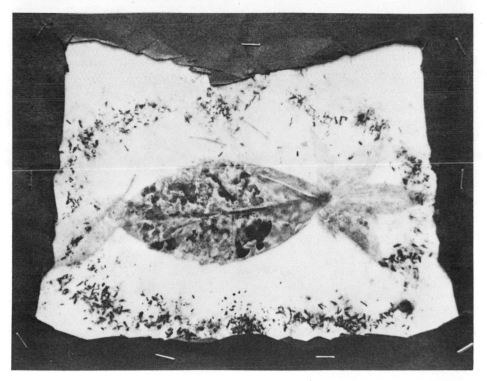

Leaves and grated crayon in waxed paper

printed on the cardboard. If the name is printed on the back, these can be used like flashcards to make an unusual learning game.

Indoor activities are more in demand as the weather becomes less favorable for outdoor enjoyment. A supply of leftover yarn and some fabric scraps form the basis for many indoor projects.

Three-strand braiding is a good beginning project for younger children. Twelve-inch lengths are good for the beginner, and once he has mastered the technique then the length can be increased. Different-colored strands simplify learning the technique and make a prettier braid. The easiest way to start the braiding is to put the three strands together and make a knot near one end. The knotted end should then be anchored in place, and a simple way to do this is

Three-strand braid,
coiled and glued
onto cardboard circle
to form a hot pad

to tape the end to something stable. During a young child's first attempt at braiding, he will sometimes forget which strand goes where and will need to be reminded and encouraged. Your patience in teaching will be rewarded by his pleasure in his achievement. When the braiding is finished, simply knot the end to hold the braid together. These first short braided strands can be used as bracelets, necklaces, or keychains by taping the ends together. Longer lengths can be used for a belt, reins for a hobby horse, or a bow on a package. They also can be coiled and glued onto a cardboard circle for an attractive hot pad.

Another use of yarn which is a little more difficult is finger knitting. This is the simplest and fastest method of knitting. It uses a chain stitch like that used in crocheting, except here you use a heavy yarn and fingers. Begin by forming a slip knot. Have the child pull a loop through the slip knot, as shown in the diagram, and pull the knot tight.

Slip knot

Pull on the long end of the yarn to reduce the size of the loop, and repeat the process again. This type of knitting goes quite rapidly, but it will take a few practice stitches before the child catches on to the method.

If your young knitter wants to change colors, simply tie on the

Finger knitting

new color and proceed as before. To finish the project, the knitted strand may be sewed into a coil or the coiled rope glued onto a circle of heavy paper. It can be used as a placemat, hot pad, or as a rug in a dollhouse.

A child's pegboard set can be converted into a simple loom on which children can learn to weave. If you do not have a pegboard set, make one from standard pegboard (any size) and ⅛-inch diameter dowels, cut into 2-inch lengths. An older child can prepare the loom but younger children will need help. Glue a row of pegs across the top and the bottom of the board. To string the loom, knot the vertical or warp yarn around the first peg and proceed according to the diagram, knotting again at the last peg.

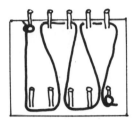

Stringing the pegboard loom

To start the weaving, have the child take a piece of yarn and begin by going over the first warp yarn and then under the next warp yarn. Continue this over-and-under procedure to the end of the board. The second piece of yarn will begin by going under the first warp yarn and then over the next. Have the child proceed with this alternating technique until the board is full. Be sure that the woven yarn pieces are pushed toward the bottom to keep the weaving tight. You can use a coarse comb for this. When the weaving is finished, the warp yarns should be carefully slipped off the pegs. To prevent raveling, the place-mat can be stitched across the loose ends (near the end warp yarns).

Cardboard weaving is a little more complex, because the weaving is done on both sides of the cardboard. The results are like an envelope, and therefore this is ideal for making a purse or toy bag. Making the

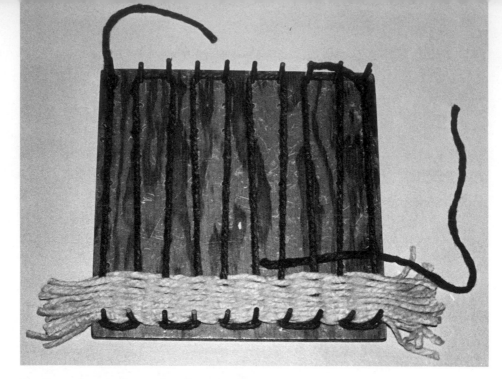

Pegboard weaving using heavy yarn

cardboard loom is also a little too complex for young children, and the loom should be prepared for them. Use a heavy, sturdy cardboard and heavy string or cord. String the warp threads on the cardboard according to directions.

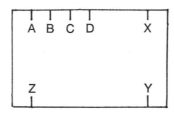

STRINGING THE CARDBOARD LOOM

1. Make a row of slots across the top of the cardboard loom about ¾″ apart. Make two slots on the bottom, one at each end.
2. Make a knot in the cord. Bring the cord through slot A (leaving the knot on the back side) and down through slot Z.

3. Go up the back and bring cord through slot A, down through slot Z, and up through A again. (There should now be two cords in this first row.)
4. Go across (on the front side) to slot B. Through B, down the back, around the bottom, and up the front through B again.
5. Go from B to C (on the back side). Through C, down the front, around, and up the back through slot C again.
6. Go from C to D (on the front) and proceed as before.
7. Continue until the stringing is completed across the card. Make two rounds through slots X and Y. Knot.

For the weaving, use any kind and color of yarn. The weaving yarn will need to be cut into lengths no longer than 4 or 5 feet, for ease in handling. Knot one end of the weaving yarn on the end warp string and let the child begin weaving over and under, continuing around both sides of the cardboard until the end of the yarn is reached. Tie on another length of yarn and let him continue weaving. Use this procedure until the cardboard is filled. Again, knot the weaving yarn to the end warp string. To remove the weaving from the loom, slip the warp strings off the top and turn the weaving inside out. For ease in carrying, the child may wish to add braided handles.

The older child who is familiar with the weaving technique may wish to try a different kind of weaving which offers a greater challenge. Nature weaving is done with other materials in addition to yarn. Try such interesting things as sticks, seedpods, long narrow leaves, weeds, and pine cones.

To weave a hanging like the one shown facing page 32 will require a loom made of twigs and cord. Wind the cord onto the twigs,

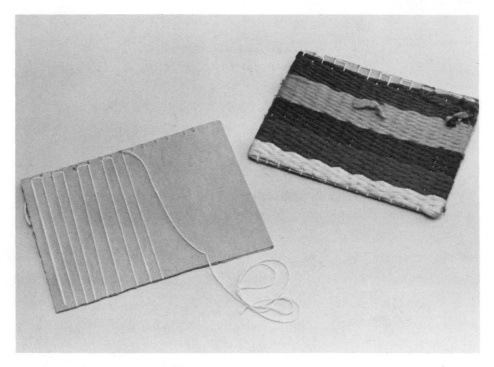

Cardboard weaving

keeping the twigs an even distance apart. After the ends are tied in place, the loom should be stretched and held in place on a board. Fiberboard works best, using large pins or pushpins for anchoring. After the loom has been secured, the weaving can begin. The weaving is the same over-and-under process used in the preceding projects, except natural materials occasionally are substituted for yarn pieces. In the case of the pine cone, use a length of yarn and weave through several of the warp threads pulling the end into place. Simply wrap the yarn around the upper scales of the pine cone and continue weaving to the end. When the hanging is completed, carefully remove the pins and hang it where it can be seen and enjoyed by everyone.

Stitchery is similar to weaving, but requires a greater degree of muscle control. While the process is more difficult to learn, it provides a greater freedom for the creativity of the child.

A beginning step is a string design. The only materials required are a piece of construction paper, some thread, and a needle. The construction paper provides a background with more body than most fabrics, and is therefore easier for a beginner to handle. Any kind of thread, embroidery floss, or lightweight string will do, the more colorful the better. Either blunt-nosed tapestry needles or the inexpensive large plastic needles work well for this.

Then the child is ready to sew. After his first stitch, the knot should be taped in place to keep it from pulling through the paper.

String design

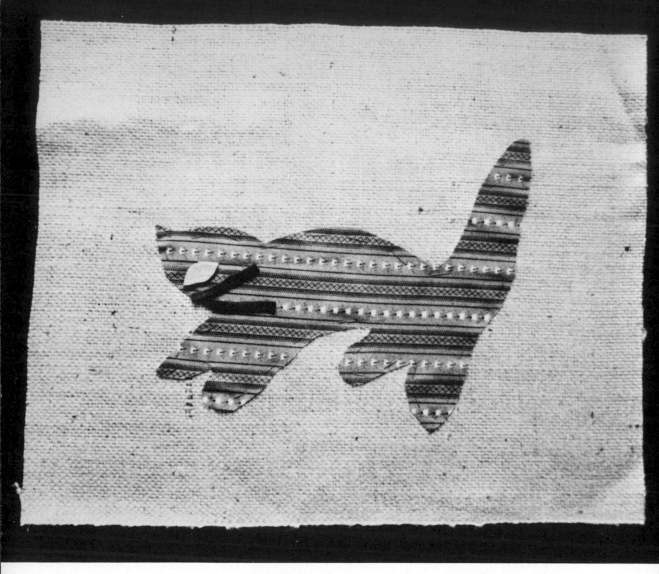

Cloth cat on burlap

The child can now create his design using any length stitch he chooses. He may use all threads of the same color or change colors, as he wishes. The important thing here is learning the technique, and some delightful designs may result from this learning process.

After the technique is learned, the next step is to begin sewing on fabric. The background fabric for the stitchery in the cat picture is burlap. It is good for beginners as it is loosely woven and therefore easy to sew through. The cat was first drawn on a fabric scrap with a felt-tip marker. It was then cut out and stitched onto the burlap. Details (eye and whiskers) were cut from felt and glued in place.

This same process, done with felt, produces something the child can actually use—a blanket for a favorite doll or teddy bear.

Small scraps of felt can be used to make little good-luck charms like the rabbit pictured. This project is a bit more complex because

Felt doll blanket

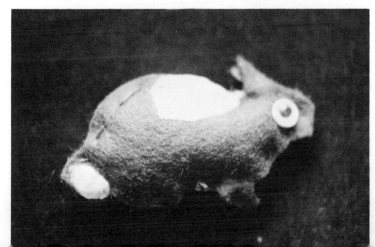

Good-luck rabbit

Cutting and gluing felt

the two pieces of cloth must be evenly matched and stuffed during the sewing. The animal shape is first drawn on the felt and two of these shapes are cut out. The two pieces are matched and then stitched together along the edge. Before the sewing is completed, the animal must be stuffed, and then stitched closed. At this point the details may be glued on, such as cotton spots and jiggly or felt eyes. Children particularly enjoy these little charms as they are easily put into a small pocket and they can take their little friend with them wherever they go.

If the child enjoys working with felt, some scraps of felt and glue can keep him occupied for quite some time. For the Indian head, the basic shape was cut out and numerous details added from a variety of

Sponge print made from outlined leaves

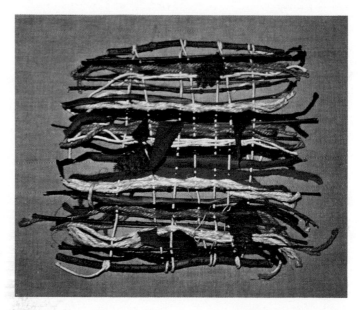

Nature weaving

Night picture

Scratch pictures

Construction paper turkey

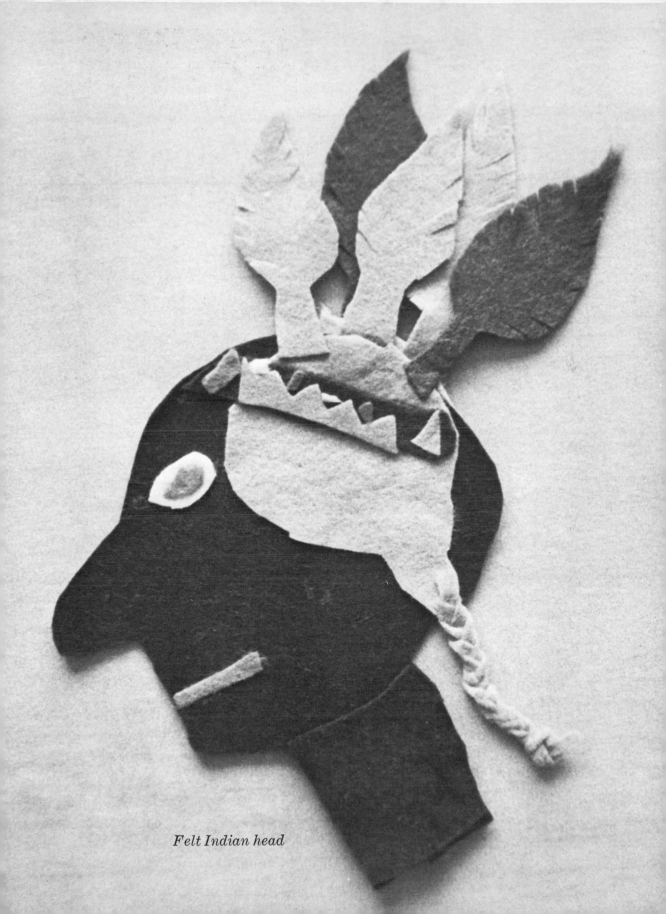

Felt Indian head

colored scraps. The possibilities for this kind of activity are applicable to any child's particular interest.

Meat tray stitchery is excellent for those who work with groups of children and have limited supplies. Each child will need a clean styrofoam meat tray, some yarn, and a needle (either plastic or tapestry). In the examples shown, the cross-stitches were done in the indented squares. The indented pattern in the bottom of the tray provided a guide for the stitching. After the stitching is completed, small construction-paper designs can be added to enhance the picture.

Children look forward to Halloween and enjoy making preparations for this special day. Halloween pictures are always great fun for children to make. For those who enjoy cutting and gluing, provide them with construction paper in Halloween colors, glue, and

Meat tray stitchery

Cut and glued construction-paper witch

scissors. Using these materials, children can create their favorite Halloween figures. Their inventiveness may result in some delightful characters.

Some of the Halloween pictures that the child has drawn can be transformed into spooky night pictures like the one shown in color opposite page 33. The picture must be a crayon drawing and an eerie effect is achieved by applying a black or dark blue wash over it. To make the wash, add a few drops of black or dark blue tempera to a glass of water—just enough to color it. Let the child paint the wash over the entire paper. He will be delighted as he sees the crayon drawing emerge through the wash. The hardest part for the child will be to let the paint dry before he proudly hangs it up.

Making a fog picture requires simple materials: construction paper, waxed paper, scissors, and glue. Because the effect desired here is that of a fog scene, provide your child with gray construction paper for the background, soft browns for the hills, and black for the trees. The sequence of layering, of the construction paper and the waxed paper, produces a three-dimensional effect.

Have the child glue a row of hills, cut from a sheet of brown paper, to the bottom edge of the gray background. He can then add one or more black trees, which should be glued in place, and cover the entire area with waxed paper. The child should then glue another set of hills and a larger black tree on top of the waxed paper. A simple way to frame the picture is to fold black construction paper over each end and staple.

Fog picture

A scratch picture is an unusual and rather complex project, but the results are most exciting. One of the best papers to use for this is a good quality white drawing paper. For a young child, provide a small sheet of paper—4″ by 4″ is good for a start. Use a small sheet because the child must press hard with a crayon to achieve a good layer of color and this can be tiring. The entire surface of the paper should be colored. The child may apply the color in random blocks or stripes—whatever suits his fancy.

When the coloring is done, cover the entire surface with a thick coat of black tempera paint and allow it to dry. After the paint has

*Halloween mask
made from newspaper*

thoroughly dried the child will need a pointed instrument (such as a nail or a fork) to scratch out his design. The scratching removes the paint and allows the colors to emerge, as shown in the picture facing page 33.

Masks are an important part of any Halloween, and it is always more fun for children to make their own. The mask in the picture is made from homemade cardboard, which requires newspapers, white glue (thinned with a little water), and paint. Be sure to cover the working surface with plenty of extra newspapers to simplify the cleanup. Each mask requires four appropriate-sized pieces of newspaper. Have the child paint the surface of one sheet with white glue. Add a second sheet, and again paint with glue. Have him do this again with the third sheet, and cover with the fourth sheet. Now he can draw the outline of the mask on the glued paper, using a felt-tip marker. The mask should then be cut out and set aside to dry. After drying he can paint his mask in wild colors with tempera paint, attach a string, and go scare his friends.

Felt-tip pens and markers are great for children. They are very colorful and so easy to use your child will undoubtedly create a number of pictures when he is first introduced to them. You may want to offer him a selection of background materials including typing paper, newspaper, and wallpaper. For variety, have him cut out and mount some of his favorite drawings.

A very special effect can be produced by adding drops of white glue to a felt-marker picture. When the drops of glue have dried, they give the appearance of snow. Not only is the picture fun to look at, but it is fun for children to feel this added texture.

Felt marker drawing

Felt marker cutouts

Snow picture

One of the most familiar symbols of Thanksgiving, the traditional American harvest festival, is the turkey. A very simple way for a child to draw a turkey is to follow the directions given in this little rhyme.

First you draw a sun,
Then add finger number 1.
Now add the other three
To keep it company.

To stand, he needs a leg,
For his toes he needs 3 pegs.
And another leg as tall,
For we don't want him to fall.

A balloon will be his wing,
Which is quite the proper thing.
His head and neck, a curvy line,
A dot for an eye will do just fine.

You'll want your turkey to be able to eat,
And so, of course, he needs a beak.
Listen to him speak,
Gobble, gobble, gobble!

Completed drawing of a turkey

A construction-paper turkey is a lovely addition to any holiday kitchen. Have the child draw the turkey shape on a large sheet of paper, and cut it out. The body feathers are formed from 1″ by 3″ strips of brown construction paper. The feathers are curled by rolling the strips around a pencil, and then gluing the end of the strip to the body of the turkey. Repeat this procedure until the whole body area is feathered. The child can cut multicolored large tail feathers and glue them in place. The head and feet details can be added by coloring or by gluing on construction paper features. (See the finished turkey in color, facing page 33.)

An empty thread spool can be transformed into a turkey. The spool will be the turkey's body, and can be painted easily with a brown felt marker if desired. Pipe cleaners, which are easy to bend, provide the head and feet. Have the child insert one pipe cleaner in the spool hole, and bend the end to form the head. Another pipe cleaner can be wrapped around the center of the spool, with the ends providing the feet. Give the child a variety of colored construction paper from which he can cut the tail feathers. These are then glued to the tail end of the turkey.

The pine cone turkey is made in very much the same way as the spool turkey. Here the pipe cleaners are wrapped around the scales of the pine cone and bent to form the head and feet. Glue the tail feathers between the pine cone scales on the appropriate end.

Spool and pine cone turkeys

Pine cone people

Pine cones can become fun characters by adding bits of paper, felt, pipe cleaners, and smaller pine cones. Your child's imagination should be his guide in creating many whimsical creatures. Any child will enjoy making these decorations, and nothing would please him more than to see them used in the centerpiece for the holiday table.

WINTER

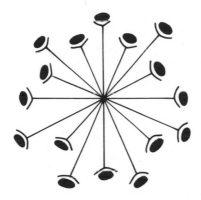

In winter, our first thoughts turn toward Christmas and the many preparations that are a part of the holiday season. Gift giving is a traditional part of Christmas and children are especially proud when they can give something that they have made themselves.

A search of the house can turn up many interesting boxes—cigar boxes, bath powder boxes, throat lozenge containers, and small candy tins. Any of these sturdy boxes can be transformed into a delightful gift. Let the child paint the outside of the box with acrylic paints. After the paint has dried, provide him with scraps of yarn, gummed paper, tissue paper, felt-tip markers, and glue. He can use any, or all, of these materials to decorate the box.

Broken eggshells can also be used to decorate a small box, such as a candy tin. In addition to the box your child will need white glue, a

Decorated boxes

paintbrush, and crunched eggshells. Put the glue in a small dish, add a few drops of water to thin the glue, making it easier for him to apply. The child should paint a small area of the box and then press the eggshells in place. He will need to repeat this process until the surface is covered. Let the box dry. There are several ways to color the eggshells. An ecru color can be obtained if the child paints the shell-covered surface with a mixture of 2 teaspoons instant coffee and 2 tablespoons water. The box on the left in the photograph was done

"Stained glass" Christmas cards

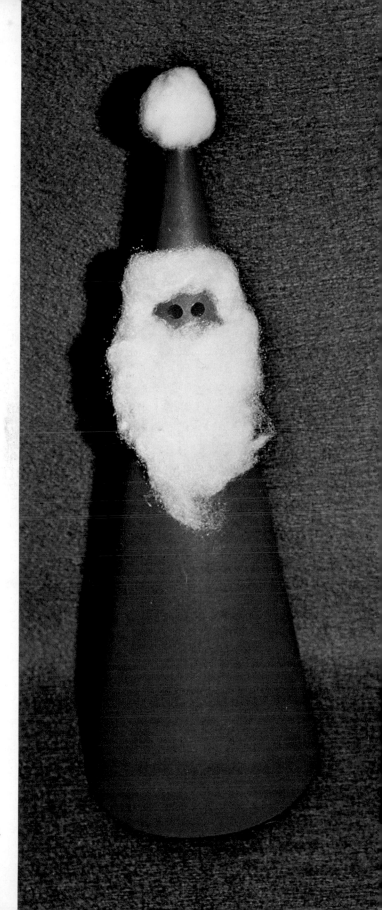

Cone Santa

Perky Penguin

Dough ornaments

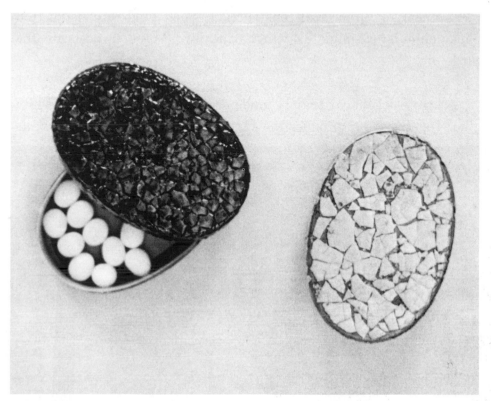

Eggshell mosaic-covered boxes

using white glue that was tinted with red food coloring. The box was covered with the tinted glue and the eggshell pieces put in place. When dry, a second coat of the red-tinted glue was applied to the entire surface. After drying, the boxes can be sprayed with varnish for a permanent finish.

Children love to make and give Christmas cards. The simplest kind is made by cutting out pictures from wrapping paper and gluing them onto a folded piece of construction paper. Colored construction paper cutouts or simple drawings can also be used to decorate the cards.

A very elegant card can be made by using felt markers and white glue. Together these produce the effect of a stained glass window, as

shown in the colorful examples facing page 48. To make the window, use a 3″ by 6″ piece of white drawing paper and cut a curved arch at the top. Let the child draw a simple scribble line with a black felt marker on the window. Now the child can color in the areas with any colors he chooses, making sure no white areas remain. At this point the glue is applied. The easiest way to do this is to have the child

Simple Christmas cards

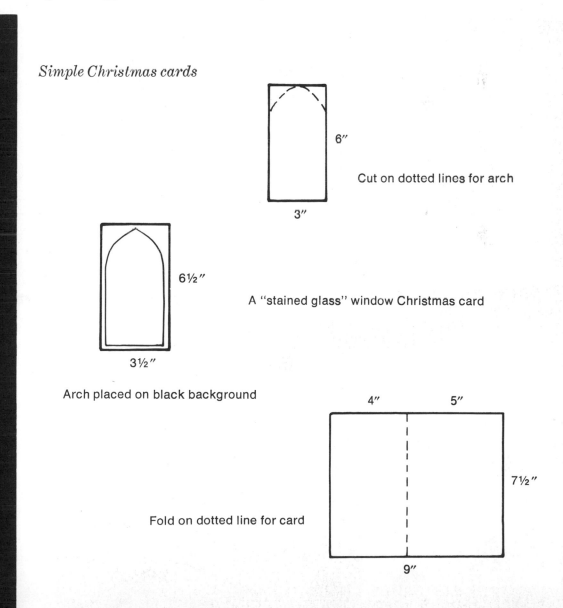

6″

Cut on dotted lines for arch

3″

6½″

A "stained glass" window Christmas card

3½″

Arch placed on black background

4″   5″

7½″

Fold on dotted line for card

9″

squeeze glue randomly over the design. Then, using one fingertip, smear the glue to cover the entire surface. Too much rubbing will cause the colors to bleed, so caution the child that once over is enough. The glue coating intensifies the colors, and gives the window a shiny surface. The window should now be laid on a piece of waxed paper to dry. When dry, the window is mounted on a piece of black construction paper 3½″ by 6½″. The framed window is then mounted on a piece of colored construction paper folded as shown below. The card color is determined by the child. Let him try his design on several different colors to see which he likes best. NOEL is printed on the extended flap and additional greetings can be written on the inside.

These cards are really beautiful and children are very proud to send them.

If in preparation for holiday baking there are walnuts to be cracked, be sure to save some of the half-shells. These can be used to make unusual tree ornaments or package decorations.

To make the turtle, cut a piece of green felt in an appropriate shape for the turtle's body, legs, and head. The turtle's "house" is half a walnut shell, which is glued in place. Two small beads are then added for his eyes.

To make a doll and cradle, stuff half a walnut shell with cotton. Tuck in a piece of fabric for a blanket, and glue a bead in place for the doll's head. Glue on pieces of yarn for hair, and if desired a face can be drawn on with a felt pen.

Either of these walnut shell creations can be a delightful tree ornament simply by gluing on a length of thread or fishing line. As a package decoration, they have the added advantage of becoming a toy after the package is opened.

Walnut shell turtle

Decorated yarn cones

Cardboard yarn cones can be the basis for some colorful table decorations. If yarn cones aren't available, they can be made from lightweight cardboard. Supply your child with scraps of fabric, yarn, and other trimmings. He will also need a brush and a small bowl of white glue which has been thinned with water. He should paint the glue on the cone and place the fabric scraps on the glued area. The yarn and trimmings are then added. Several of these set in a bed of pine boughs are a most cheerful holiday table decoration.

A red construction-paper cone can easily become a charming Santa. Glue on some cotton for the beard and another small piece to frame his face. Add two small blue circles for his eyes and a cotton ball to top off his hat. This Santa is shown in color opposite page 48.

A paper-bag penguin is fun to make and even more fun to look at. The materials needed are: a white lunch bag, a sheet of black construction paper, and small pieces of orange and white construction paper. Have the child fill the bag about two-thirds full of loosely crumpled newspaper. Close the top and fold over once. Cut the black features according to the pattern shown. If the child is very young an adult should cut the beak open. Coat the body area with glue, as shown in the second figure. Attach this to the back of the paper bag, inserting the fold under the beak. To finish the penguin, add two white paper circles for the eyes, using felt markers to make the pupils. The feet are two strips of orange construction paper (each strip is 1½″ by 3″). The child can form the toes by snipping out two triangles from

A paper bag penguin

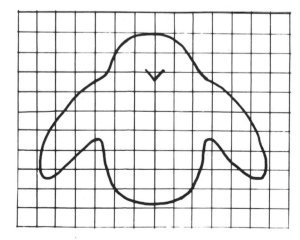

Cut shape from 9″ by 12″ paper
(1 square equals 1 square inch).

Apply glue to lined area.

the front edge. Glue the feet to the bottom of the bag, and Perky Penguin is ready to go. Perky also can be an unusual wrapping for a child's gift, and in that case the gift is substituted for the crumpled newspaper. (See the color picture that faces page 49.)

Using macaroni, waxed paper, and white glue your child can make some very lovely ornaments. These lacy ornaments can be used as Christmas tree decorations, but also make a lovely window or wall decoration, or add an elegant touch to a gift package.

To make the ornaments, spread a piece of waxed paper on the child's working surface—this will allow him to remove the designs easily when they are dry. The procedure is very simple: pour a small amount of white glue onto the waxed paper, let the child dip the edges of the macaroni into the glue and form his design. He may find tweezers will aid in handling the macaroni pieces.

This idea can be carried one step further, by adding background materials. Pieces of cut Plexiglas allow more flexibility in making open designs. Also try sheet cork or disposable aluminum pans, both of which can be cut with scissors, and colored with felt markers.

By using the dough recipe on page 13, children can create dozens of Christmas decorations. After the decorations have been shaped and baked according to the recipe directions, they can then be painted. Tempera, craft, and acrylic paints all work well. If desired, glitter can be sprinkled on while the paint is still wet. Attach thread or yarn for a hanger. (See picture facing page 49.)

Some very inexpensive ornaments can be made from disposable aluminum pans. The only additional items needed are a pair of

Macaroni ornaments with a variety of background materials

Dough snowman

Metal ornaments

scissors and colored felt markers. The child can draw a shape or trace around a favorite cookie cutter to form a cutting line. This light-weight aluminum is easily cut with scissors and does not produce a sharp edge as one might think. After the shapes are cut out, the child may color them with the felt markers. To hang the ornaments, punch a hole and attach a piece of thread or fishing line.

When Christmas is over, it is time to put away our treasures for next year. Usually things like Christmas cards and used wrapping paper will be thrown away. Don't do it! Save some of these pretty discards and give them to your child to use. After he tires of looking at the pictures, have him cut out some of his favorites and make a collage like the one shown.

A particularly interesting way to use old Christmas cards is to construct a ball. The child will need to cut 3½-inch circles out of the cards. If you have a glass or a cup that is about 3½ inches in diameter, this will provide him with a pattern to trace around. He will need 20 circles to form the ball. Each of these circles needs to be folded. To do this folding, the child uses a cardboard triangle that is 3 inches on each side. The triangle is placed on the circle and the parts of the circle that extend beyond it are folded up. After he has folded all the circles, he is ready to staple them together. Match the folded edge of one circle with the folded edge of a second circle and staple them together. Follow the list of steps to construct the ball.

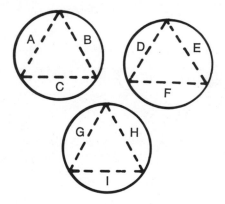

A Christmas card ball

1. Staple sides B and D together.
2. Staple sides C and G together.
3. Staple sides F and H together.
4. Continue adding circles until the ball is complete.

Dough animals

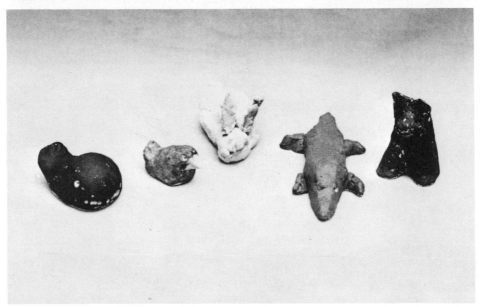

Painted dough animals

The weather in the months right after Christmas means more indoor activities. This would be a good time for your child to explore the animal kingdom.

By using the dough recipe on page 13, your child can create his own animals—either real or imaginary. After they have been shaped, bake according to the directions.

Your child may wish to paint his animals, and acrylic paints work very well for this. Perhaps an animal your child has made is not a stand-up kind. If he particularly likes it and wants to keep it safe, he may wish to mount it. The flat side of the animal can be glued to a small board which has been painted.

Many children are very fond of animal-shaped cookies. And a box of them provides a quick way of adding to an animal collection. They can be painted in a variety of colors using acrylic paints. Caution your child not to eat the painted cookies; however, the box is sure to yield many broken pieces for the artist to eat.

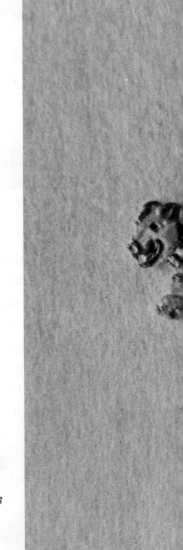

Painted cookies

Jointed animals can be made easily from construction paper, felt markers, and paper fasteners. The child should first draw the pieces on the paper—a head, body, and four legs. This may take a little practice, since he isn't used to drawing animals in pieces. With felt-tip markers, the eyes, nose, mouth, and any other details are added. Next

the child should cut out the pieces and put them together with the paper fasteners. The fasteners act as joints, so that parts of the animal can be moved, thus allowing the animal to walk or even do tricks.

Children will enjoy making soap-filled animals. For these one needs art foam, which is available in a variety of colors in hobby

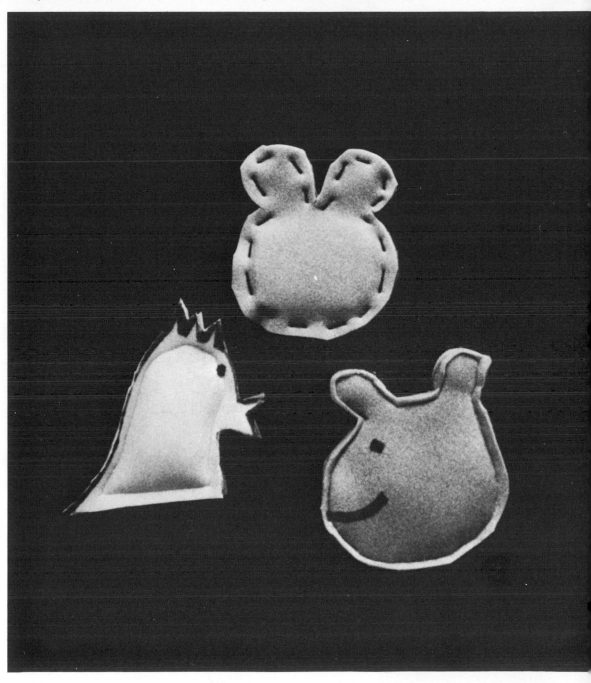

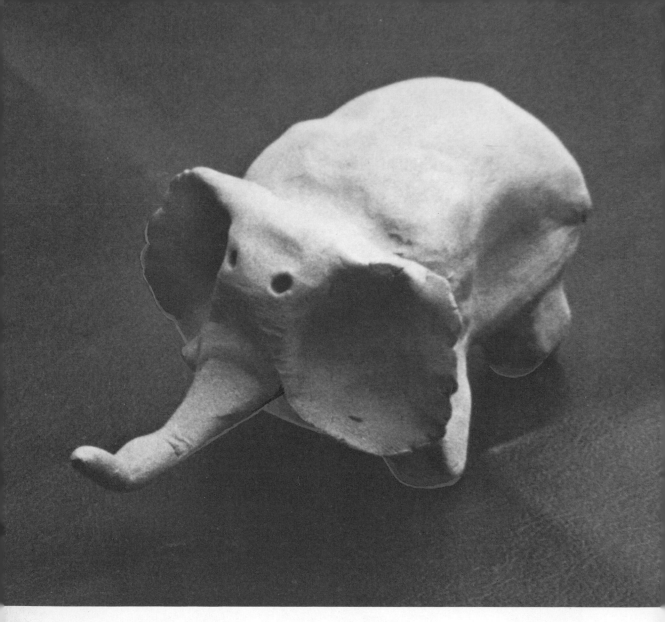

Big-eared elephant

shops. The child should first draw the desired shape on the foam with a permanent felt marker, and cut out two of these shapes. The animals are then stitched either by machine or by hand. Before the stitching is completed, the center of the animal is filled with soap, either a small bar or leftover chips from soap carving, and stitched closed. These make unusual washcloths and will surely make bathtime more fun.

Modeling or carving can be a challenging and rewarding experience for a child. The big-eared elephant was modeled from self-hardening clay. There are many kinds of clays available, including modeling clay, potter's clay (which needs to be fired), and self-hardening clay, which dries hard without firing. You may wish to let your child experiment with any or all of these.

If carving is more to your child's liking, soap is a good beginning medium. Use a fresh bar of soap, as it is soft and won't crack easily.

Soap carvings

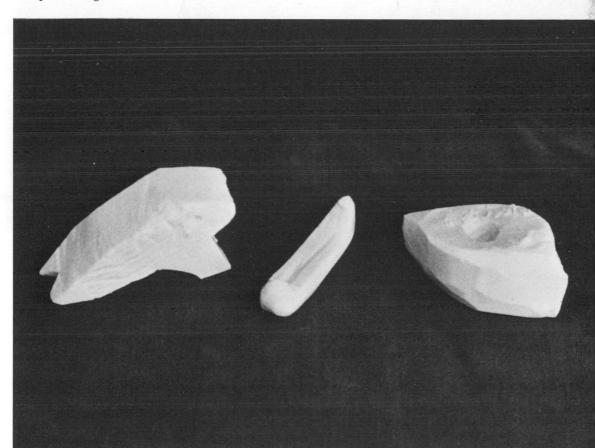

Vermiculite bear

Plastic knives work well and are the safest tool for carving, particularly for young children. A simple beginning project is a boat. After some practice, your child may want to try something a little more difficult such as an animal. These carved soap figures are fun for kids to use at bathtime.

A combination of plaster of paris and vermiculite was used to make the substance from which the bear was carved. The advantage of this substance is that it can be made in any size block desired and is very easy to carve. Use equal parts of dry plaster of paris and vermiculite, and add enough water to make it the consistency of thick cream. Pour this mixture into an appropriate-size milk carton and let it sit until it has hardened. When the substance has set, peel away the milk carton and let your child begin carving.

This is an excellent medium for children, because the carving doesn't have to be done with a sharp knife. A table knife works well, as do spoons, forks, and other kitchen implements. Adults will also enjoy working with this medium, as a sharp knife can be used to produce detailed sculpture.

The procedure for papier-mâché work requires newspapers and wallpaper (wheat) paste. If your child does not like to get his hands dirty this is not the project for him.

First of all, cover the work area with several layers of newspaper. Mix the wallpaper paste according to the directions on the

Papier-mâché cat

package. Tear newspapers in strips about 1 inch wide. The cat in the picture used a blown-up balloon for the body shape. The child starts by dipping a strip of newspaper in the paste mixture and wrapping it around the balloon. He continues this process until he has several (4 or 5) layers of newspaper strips on the balloon. Set it aside and let it dry. The body is now complete. To finish the cat, he can pop the balloon with a pin and remove it if possible. He then tapes crumpled balls of newspaper in place to serve as the bases for making the head, legs, and tail. He should cover these with more paste-dipped strips, rounding out features as desired. After the cat has dried, it can be

Dinosaur diorama

painted with any type of paint. This cat makes a delightful addition to your child's animal collection.

A nice home for a group of small animals can be constructed from a cardboard box. The first step is to remove the front and top of the box. First, the child draws in the background scene. With acrylic or tempera paint he can paint the scene in the desired colors. Then the special effects can be added such as rocks, dried grass, and animals. When finished, the diorama is as much fun to play with as it is to look at. This idea is adaptable to most any animal group— jungle, desert, prehistoric, or domestic.

74

One of the last special days in winter is Valentine's Day.

A heart-shaped beanbag makes an unusual Valentine for a favorite person. The child should cut two heart shapes from red felt.

Valentine beanbags

Valentines

A small white bow is then stitched or glued to one of the hearts. The two heart shapes must be machine-stitched together (an adult will have to help here). Before the stitching is completed, the beanbag

must be filled. The filling can be dry beans or unpopped popcorn. After filling, complete the stitching. By substituting cotton for the filling, this makes a lovely pincushion.

A collection of red and white construction paper, some paper doilies, and glue can be combined to form a great variety of Valentines. The heart shapes should be predrawn in a number of different sizes for the child to cut out. He can arrange or stack them however he desires. One way to put two hearts together is to attach a "spring." To make the spring, accordion-fold a piece of construction paper, ½" by 2". Glue it in the center, between the two hearts. For variety your child may want to add gummed Valentine stickers, parts of old Valentine cards, and perhaps an "I Love You."

SPRING

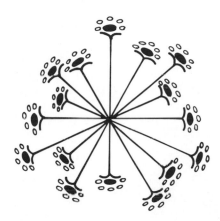

Spring is a time for new activities, both indoor and out. The appearance of new leaves, a refreshing change in the weather, and the Easter holiday are all important aspects of this season.

The Easter holiday is one that children always enjoy preparing for. One unusual decoration which your children would have fun making is a fabric bubble egg.

The bubble eggs require small fabric scraps and wallpaper (wheat) paste. Blown-up balloons provide a base on which to form the eggs. The size of the egg is determined by the size of the balloon used. The fabric scraps are dipped into the paste mixture and applied to the balloon, leaving an appropriate-size opening on one side. Be sure that the child covers all remaining areas with the fabric pieces. The pieces should overlap each other, particularly on a large-size egg, to add the strength to keep the balloon shape. After the balloon has

been covered, set it on a piece of waxed paper to dry thoroughly. After drying, pop the balloon and remove it. In the large egg, the balloon may stick to the sides. In this case, just wait a while as the balloon will gradually pull itself loose.

To finish, fill the bottom of the egg with Easter grass and add other Easter decorations. Little feathery chicks and colored jelly beans are just right for the small-size bubble, while the large-size egg can hold items such as dyed eggs and toy chicks or bunnies. (The large egg is shown in color opposite page 96.)

Decorating eggs

Decorated blown-out eggshells are simple to make, but add a very special touch to your Easter decorations. To blow out an egg, hold the egg in one hand and poke a hole about one-quarter inch in diameter in one end with a heavy pin or a very small nail. Hold the egg over a bowl and punch a hole in the other end. Then blow the egg into the bowl.

The eggs shown in color facing page 96 were made by decorating blown-out eggshells with colored felt markers. Because these eggshells are fragile caution children to handle them gently. Simply provide both felt-tip markers and pens in a variety of colors and let the child create his own design. To cover the holes in the ends of the eggs, glue on small circles of sheer fabric, such as organdy. If necessary, felt pens can be used to color the fabric where it overlaps the design. Attach a piece of thread for hanging. Now, the egg can be sprayed with lacquer or varnish. Spinning the egg as it is sprayed will insure an even coat.

Eggshells can be decorated at any other time of year using appropriate designs.

Blown-out eggshells can also be turned into egg characters with bits of paper, felt, and pipe cleaners. This photograph shows several possibilities—just to give you a start. To help the eggs stand, form a collar of construction paper to fit around the bottom part of the eggs. By adding a name to the collar these make delightful place cards for an Easter dinner.

If your family traditionally dyes eggs for Easter, be sure to save some of the colored shells for use in an eggshell mosaic. A small box covered with the various colored shell pieces is a lovely Mother's Day gift. Directions for this process are given on page 47.

Egg characters

Chalk and sheet eggs

Another kind of egg decoration is a chalk and sheet egg. Cut an egg shape, in the desired size, from lightweight cardboard. Lay a piece of old sheeting, either white or pastel, over the cardboard egg. Using a paintbrush, have the child paint the sheeting with liquid starch. Make sure he thoroughly saturates the area of the sheet covering the cardboard egg. Now the egg is ready to be decorated. Using chalk, the child draws his design on the wet cloth. The decorating is very exciting for children, as the moist starch brings out the vivid color of the chalk. When the decorated egg has dried, trim the excess sheeting from around the edges of the cardboard egg shape.

Because these eggs are such fun, children will probably want to do several. A group of these would make a colorful Easter decoration for their room.

Charming Easter baskets can be made from half-pint milk cartons. The cartons should be washed and opened at the top. To form the upper edges of the baskets, have the child trim the tops of the cartons as he chooses. The photograph shows several ways of cutting these upper edges. The baskets can then be painted. Water-base wall paint

Easter baskets

works best here, as it adheres well to the cartons and is washable. Pipe cleaner handles can be added if desired. The baskets are then ready to be filled. The rabbit basket is made in much the same way. Remove three of the upper sides at the fold line, and cut rabbit-ear shapes in the remaining side. Let the child glue cotton on the outside of the carton. Felt or construction-paper features can be added for the rabbit's face. Children enjoy making and giving these soft Easter bunny baskets.

Hinged baskets are also made from half-pint milk cartons. For these, the cartons should be rinsed out and dried and then the tops

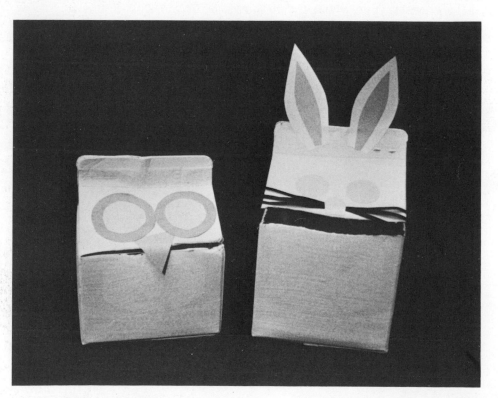

Hinged Easter baskets

stapled shut again. The child can now paint the cartons. In order to make the hinged top, the carton should be cut on three sides along the fold line (an adult should do this). The fourth side serves as a hinge allowing the basket to open and close. The carton can now be decorated with construction-paper details to make any character the child wishes.

The milk carton baskets can be used for May Day or Mother's Day. Filled with flowers, either wild or from the garden, these make a simple but delightful gift for a child to give. (See color picture facing page 97.)

A doily flower bouquet is an unusual gift. Your child will need a small vase, several paper doilies, fine wire, white glue, and scissors. Let him cut small flowers from a paper doily, and glue them onto a length of fine wire. He can then arrange his flowers in the vase. This idea is particularly nice as a remembrance for a shut-in or during the months when fresh flowers are not readily available.

Dough can be used to make a lovely spring gift like the one shown in the picture. Let the child shape the various parts of the flower from the dough (recipe on page 13). He should assemble the total flower on the baking sheet. After the flowers have been baked, they can be left in a natural state or painted with acrylic paints. To finish this project, the dough flowers are glued onto a sturdy surface. Heavy colored cardboard or a piece of wood that has been painted or covered with felt works well. A gummed hanger attached to the back completes the gift.

Dough flowers

Yarn picture

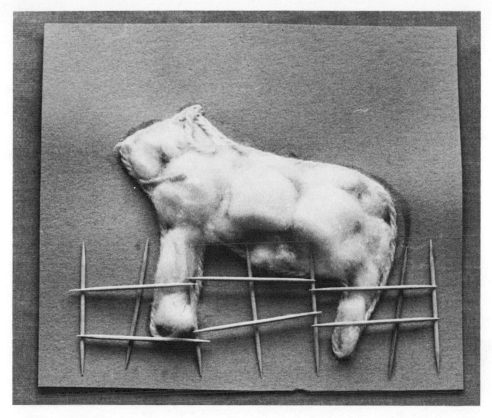

Lamb collage

A yarn flower picture requires only construction paper, yarn, crayons, and glue. To make the picture, the child should first draw the flower on the paper, using a crayon. These crayon lines are then covered with yarn which is glued in place. After he has completed this step, the child may leave the picture as it is, or he may solidly fill in any of the enclosed areas with more yarn. Colored construction paper combined with yarn in varied colors makes an attractive picture to give on Mother's Day.

For a variety in texture the child may wish to include other materials in his yarn picture, such as shown in the lamb collage. Here the yarn shape was filled in with cotton balls to suggest the lamb's wool, and a toothpick fence added to complete the picture.

A mosaic, such as the one shown facing page 97, is done in a manner similar to the lamb except that several kinds of beans and seeds are used to provide the color and texture. In order to support the weight of the beans and seeds, a lightweight cardboard should be used for the backing. This method offers more challenge for the child as he can draw the picture on the cardboard and fill it in, or compose it freely as he goes along.

Bookmarks

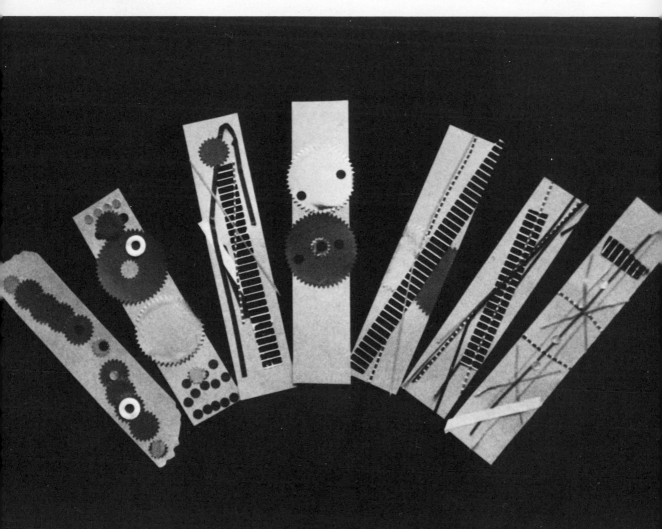

Stationery printing done using a raw cut potato

Simple bookmarks make a useful gift for any occasion. The materials needed are lightweight cardboard and gummed decorations. There is a great variety of this type of decoration available: gummed dots, line tape, labels, and notary seals—all of which come in various colors. You may wish to take your child to the stationery store to choose several kinds that he particularly likes. Cut the cardboard in 2″ by 7″ rectangles and let the child apply the decorations in any design he chooses.

Your child can transform any kind of plain ordinary paper into something special by adding a printed design. The materials needed for printing are: any kind of plain paper and envelopes, water-base

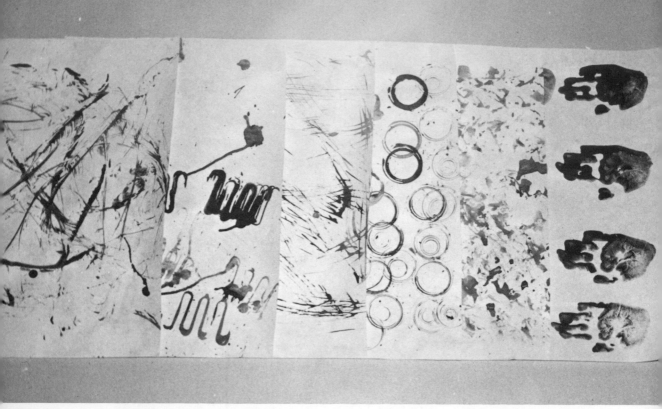

A variety of printed wrapping paper

paint, and something to make the design. Either tempera or acrylic paints work very well for printing. If tempera paint is used, add a little white glue. This gives the paint a better adhesive quality and a slight sheen when dry. The implement used for printing can be anything your child wishes such as: sponges, buttons, silverware, potato mashers, rubber bands, or string. To obtain a particular design use a hand, a foot, cookie cutters, fruit halves, or a shape cut into a raw potato or an eraser.

The procedure is very simple. Mix the paint in a small shallow container, and let the child dip whatever he is printing with into the paint. He then presses it onto the paper, and repeats this as often as he desires. Let the paint dry thoroughly.

Printed stationery is a very useful gift and printed wrapping paper adds a very personal touch to a package.

Butterfly pins

A crawly caterpillar can be made from brightly colored construction paper. Each caterpillar requires four sheets of 9″ by 12″ paper. Cut each sheet into three strips, 4″ by 9″ each. The child assembles the caterpillar in the same fashion as a paper chain, alternating the colors. To finish his crawly creature, have him cut eyes and antennae from black construction paper and glue them in place. The finished caterpillar is shown in color facing page 97.

An attractive butterfly pin can be made from a paper bag and white glue. The first step is to have the child find a picture of a butterfly that appeals to him. He will then need to draw or trace the butterfly and color it as he wishes with fine-tipped felt pens. The next step is to prepare the backing. The child will need four pieces of paper bag in an appropriate size for the butterfly he is using. He then should

glue the four pieces together, one on top of the other. Glue the butterfly on the top of the glued paper bags—being careful not to smear the
color—and cut around the edge of the butterfly. The easiest way to
shape the butterfly's wings is to lay it on the bottom of an egg carton
and push the body down between the cups, thus forcing the wings up.

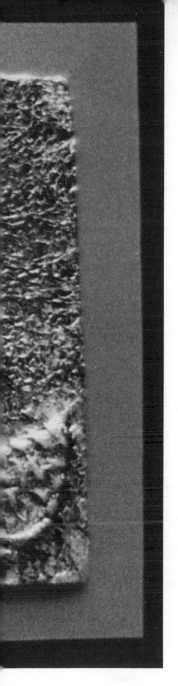

Foil picture

When the butterfly is dry, he can add antennae, tape a small safety pin to the back, and then spray with varnish for a shiny finish.

An everyday item such as aluminum foil can be used to create an unusual picture in relief. The background can be any kind of heavy cardboard, any size. Onto the cardboard, let the child place a number of items such as nails, washers, bolts, straws, beans, yarn, or cardboard shapes, to create his design. The design pieces should then be glued in place and allowed to dry. Then take a sheet of aluminum foil which is 2 inches larger on each side than the background. The child can loosely crumple the foil to wrinkle it, and then gently spread it out. He should apply water-thinned white glue over the design and the cardboard. Starting at the top of the design, he applies the foil, and gently pushes it with his fingers into all the crevices and over the upraised areas. He should slowly work down toward the bottom of the design. When this is finished, bend the edges of the foil to the back of the cardboard, glue them down, and let dry.

He can add depth and highlights to his picture by applying an india ink solution. The solution is made by adding 8 drops of liquid soap to 1 ounce of india ink. Stir the mixture gently to prevent bubbles from forming and let him paint the mixture over the foil. Let the picture dry for at least 24 hours. When dry, he can use a soft cloth and brush gently over the raised areas to give it a burnished look. This brings out the highlights of the design. The finished picture can then be mounted on colored cardboard for hanging.

Most everyone enjoys hearing wind chimes, and if you don't have any, spring is an ideal time to make some. An inexpensive way for a child to make wind chimes is to use melted disposable plastic glasses. Disposable glasses come in a variety of colors; the chimes in the picture were made from yellow and clear glasses. Be sure to purchase a large quantity of glasses for this purpose, as it is such fun to do your child won't want to quit. To make the rings, he should take several glasses, turn them upside down, and tap the bottom gently with a

Large fabric bubble egg

Decorated eggshells

May Day basket

Bean and seed mosaics

Paper caterpillar

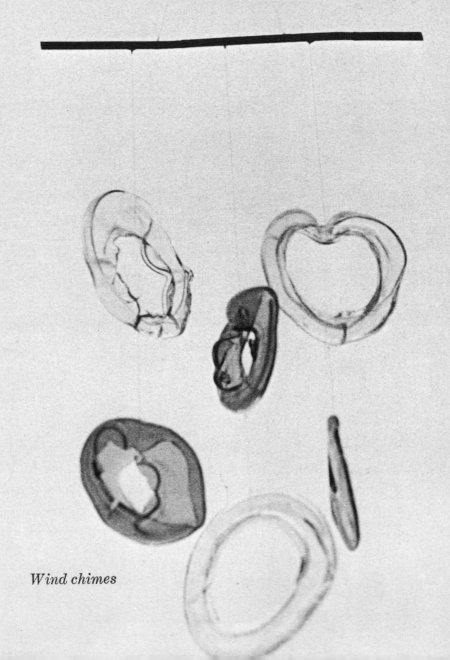

Wind chimes

Tying a wind chime

hammer to produce several cracks. Have him place the cracked glasses upside down on a foil-covered cookie sheet, spacing them several inches apart. Put them into a 350°F oven for several minutes. If you have a glass-doored oven be sure to turn on your oven light so everyone can watch! You will see each glass gradually collapse, forming a ring.

Wind chimes in an outdoor setting

Remove the cookie sheet from the oven and let it sit until the rings are cool enough to handle. Remove the rings and attach them to a dowel or bamboo stake with clear fishing line. They should be hung close enough together to allow them to touch each other.

The decorative piece hanging above the dowel was made by laying a small glass on its side and melting it. The bottom does not have to be cracked for this. Attach a fishing line loop for hanging.

SUMMER

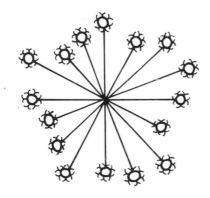

There are great numbers of colorful birds to be seen during the summer months, and what better way to greet summer than by making a bird mobile. Perhaps there is one bird that particularly appeals to your child and he may wish to use that bird's color combination in making his bird mobile.

He will first need to draw the bird body shape on a piece of construction paper. He will also need to draw two wing shapes. These shapes can now be cut out and the wings stapled onto the body. The wings should be folded upward to give the appearance of flying. Construction-paper beak and eye, and a thread for hanging complete the mobile.

Children enjoy drawing animals and an unusual way to use some of the drawings is to make stuffed animals. The child can choose one

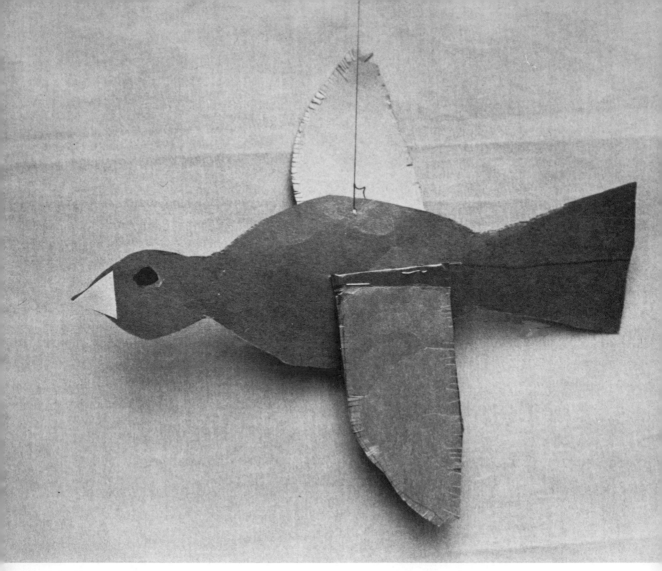

Bird mobile

of his favorite animal drawings and cut out two of the shapes. He can decorate them using felt-tip markers or construction-paper scraps. Hold the two shapes together and have him punch holes around the edges. Yarn can then be laced through the holes. Before the lacing is completed the animal should be stuffed with crumpled pieces of newspapers and then the lacing finished. These stuffed animals can be made of felt, stuffed with cotton, and used as pillows. See the examples in color opposite page 112.

Animals of a more fanciful nature can be easily made from instant papier-mâché. This type of papier-mâché is made from a pre-packaged mixture to which only water is added. The mixture is generally available in hobby shops. This type of papier-mâché is similar to clay in texture; however, when dried it is quite hard and light-weight. Chenille sticks, beads, and pipe cleaners can be used for the creatures' features. These should be added before the mâché has dried. After drying, the mâché can be painted if desired. Children can use their imaginations to make any kind of creature they wish.

Papier-mâché creatures

Mother and baby turtles

The turtles pictured would make a delightful addition to your child's menagerie. The mother turtle's shell is made from two paper plates. The child can paint the bottom sides of these plates in any design he wishes, using tempera paints. The feet, head, and tail are cut from construction paper and glued to the rim of one of the paper plates. The second plate is then glued in place.

The baby turtle is a cup from an egg carton. The construction-paper features are glued on the bottom edge. This turtle can also be painted if the child wishes.

Cracker boxes, a paper towel tube, construction paper, and some imagination can be used to create a movable circus train. Any kind or size of cracker box can be used for either the engine or car. The more boxes you have, the longer the train will be.

To begin making the train, let the child paint the boxes with latex paint, using any color available. After the paint has dried, he is ready to assemble the engine. The one in the photograph is made using one whole box for the engine and half of a second box to form the cab. The smokestack is a piece of paper towel tube. Construction-paper details are added, including smoke clouds which are glued to a piece of fine wire anchored inside the smokestack. The animal car is made by removing sections from both sides of a box, then adding strips of construction paper to form the bars. After the circus car has been decorated, the wheels are added. The wheels are made from light-weight cardboard circles which are attached with paper fasteners, allowing them to turn. To complete the train, the child may add toy or construction-paper animals. The finished train is shown opposite page 112.

There are a variety of puppets that your child can make to use in putting on a backyard show to entertain his friends.

Perhaps the easiest puppets a child can make are from felt-pen drawings. These drawings are cut out and a small ring of paper at-

Finger puppets

tached to the back. He simply slips his fingers inside the ring to make his finger puppet perform.

A shoe box without the lid will provide a theater for the show. First the child can paint the box and when the paint is dry, cut an

Shoe box theater

opening in the bottom for the front of the stage. A piece of fabric is glued inside the box for a curtain. Now, let the show begin.

Clothespin puppets are particularly amusing because they can "talk." Each puppet requires one spring-type clothespin and a cork.

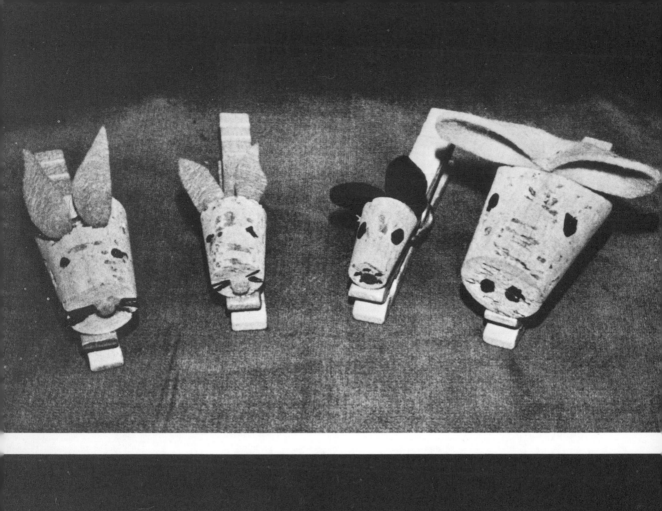

The cork is glued to one side of the clothespin. Identifying features are added using felt scraps and felt markers. By pinching the clothespin, the child can make the puppets talk.

Fuzzy finger puppets are a very special project which children will thoroughly enjoy. A 3-inch square of fuzzy fabric will be needed for each puppet. Fold the fabric, with the fuzzy sides together, and stitch along the edge, forming a tube. Sew one end of the tube closed and turn right side out. To finish his furry friend, the child can add a felt tongue and jiggly eyes. Children enjoy cuddling these creatures as well as playing with them.

Summer is the best time for water play, whether it be in rain puddle, swimming pool, or bathtub. While splashing in the water is

Sponge and cork boats

Fuzzy puppets

great fun for a while, your child may wish to add some toys to his games. A simple boat race could be held in a rain puddle using leaves as ships. More elaborate ships can be made using a variety of household materials. The young shipbuilder may begin by using sponges, either whole or cut into various shapes. He can also make a simple raft out of a styrofoam meat tray or by gluing popsicle sticks together and adding sails or a string for pulling. Cork stoppers, the larger the better, make good boats. On smaller-sized corks the child will first have to hammer a small galvanized nail into the bottom of the cork for balast. He is now ready to add sails to the upper portion of the boat.

Meat tray, sponge, and coconut shell boats

This can be done easily by putting appropriate-sized pieces of paper on a toothpick—scraps of wrapping paper make delightfully colored sails.

As your child progresses in the art of boat building, he may want to try new materials, such as eggshells, coconut shells, walnut shell halves, and citrus fruit halves. Each of these boats will need a small lump of clay on the inside to hold the mast and sails. (Walnut shell boats are shown facing page 113.)

These are a few suggestions for starters. Your child will undoubtedly discover new materials he can use in making boats.

Lemon half and eggshell boats

Glued rocks

Painted rocks decorated with felt and fabric

Stuffed animals

Cracker box train

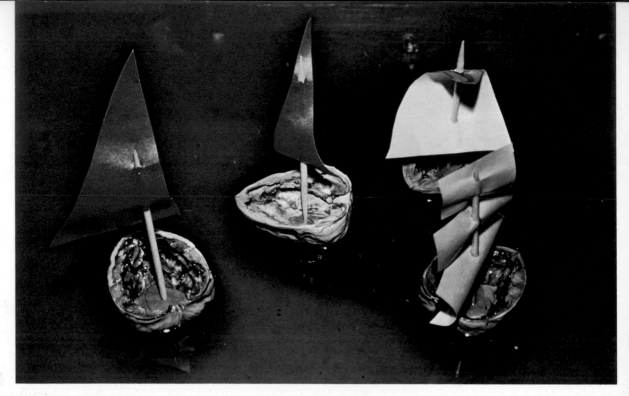

Walnut shell boats

Crayon batik

Children are born collectors when it comes to rocks. Some children enjoy making a collection to study the different kinds of rocks they have found. While some of the rocks will go into their collection, there will be others that they may wish to treat in another manner.

By gluing some of the rocks together the child can make a rock sculpture. Felt markers can be used to add small details.

Color can be added to rocks by painting them with acrylic paints. The child may wish to paint a picture or a random design. Yarn, felt, or fabric scraps can be added to give more character to the painted rocks. Your child will have great fun creating his rock family.

Driftwood keychains

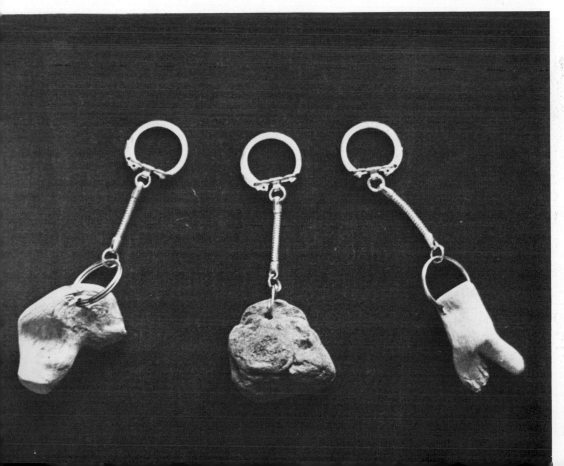

Sand candles

Perhaps your child has some small pieces of driftwood, found during a visit to the seashore, or given to him by a friend. These can be used to make very unusual keychains. If the driftwood piece is too large, a child can easily saw this soft wood into smaller sections. The cut edges should be lightly sanded to make them smooth. Children will like to do this, as the sanding goes very quickly.

An adult will now have to drill a small hole through one end of the driftwood piece so the key ring can be attached. When completed, this makes an ideal Father's Day gift for Dad or Grandfather.

Sand candles can be made at the beach or in a child's sandbox. All that is necessary for making the candles is damp sand, paraffin that has been melted with crayons to give it color, and a wick. Let the child dig a small hole in the damp sand, and prepare the wick by winding one end around a pencil or stick. Guide the child in placing the stick across the top of the hole to support the wick. An adult should then pour the melted wax in the hole; then the candle is left to harden. When the wax has hardened, the candle can be removed and the excess sand brushed away from the sides. After doing this once or twice, your child will see the possibilities for making many exciting and unusual-shaped candles.

The many different-shaped leaves available during the summer months can be used in making some unusual leaf prints.

The prints in the picture were made using self-hardening clay and small leaves. This type of clay is particularly nice to work with

Leaf prints in self-hardening clay

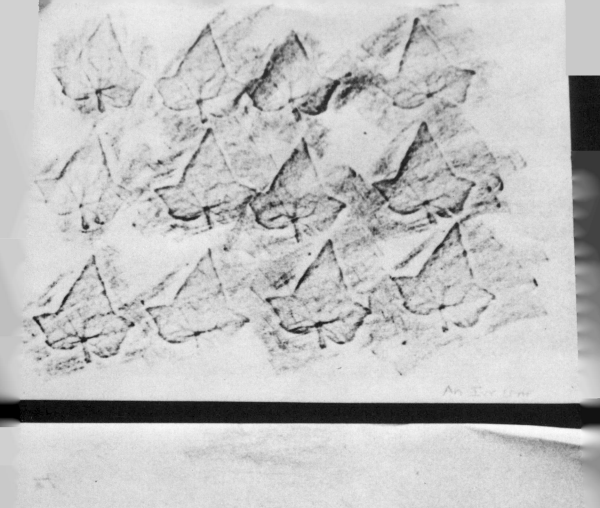

An Ivy leaf

A lemon leaf.

as it does not need to be fired and is readily available in hobby shops. To make the print, the child should press a small lump of clay flat. He may shape the outer edges if he chooses. He then presses the leaf onto the smooth surface of the clay, and then gently removes the leaf, leaving the pattern in the clay. If he plans to hang the print, he should make a small hole near the top with a toothpick. When the clay has hardened, a piece of yarn can be added for the hanger.

Children will have great fun doing crayon rubbings of leaves as they like to watch the shapes emerge as the crayon is rubbed over the paper. The only materials required are leaves, lightweight paper, and a brightly colored crayon. To do a crayon rubbing, the leaf is placed under the paper and then the crayon is rubbed over the paper in the area covering the leaf. If your child does several rubbings using different leaves, he may want to identify them and make a collection of this type of leaf print.

Leaf rubbing

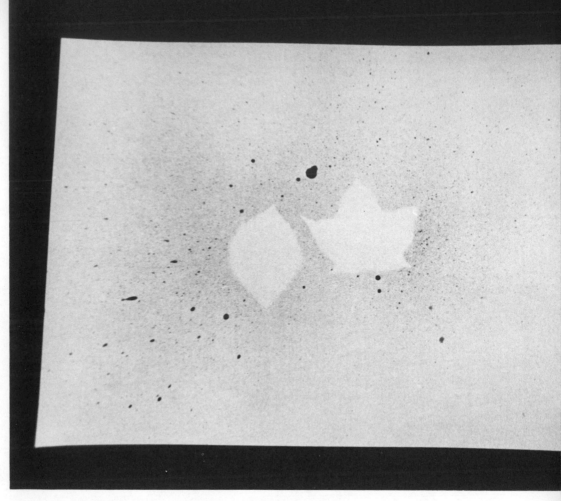

Spatter paintings

Spatter painting is a more complex method of obtaining a leaf print. To make this kind of print, the leaf is placed on the paper and the paint is spattered over the entire surface. When the leaf is removed, the blank area it covered forms the print.

To get the spatter effect, dip a toothbrush into tempera paint and gently brush it over a piece of screen (window screening is about the right size mesh) or an old sieve. The child can choose any kind or color of paper he wishes, and should choose a color of paint that is contrasting or complimentary to the color of paper chosen. These spatter prints make lovely delicate note cards.

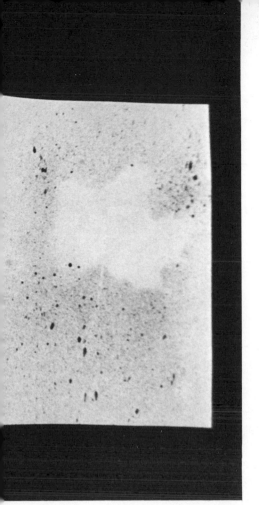

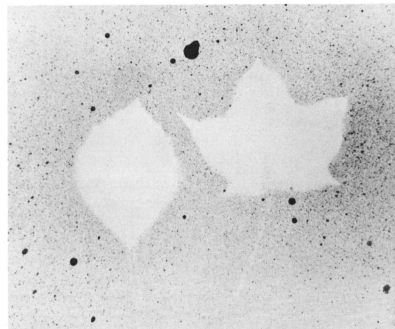

There are two other methods of printing that require special paper. The first one uses blueprint paper and the other method requires photographic paper. These special papers can sometimes be purchased inexpensively when they have become outdated. Both of these papers are light-sensitive and should be covered and handled carefully to allow as little light as possible to reach the paper. Each paper requires a special solution in order to fix the print and to prevent fading. Blueprint paper must be dipped in household ammonia and the photographic paper requires a fixing solution which can be purchased in dry form at a camera shop. The solution should be put in a flat glass or plastic pan, large enough to accommodate the piece of paper being used.

Cut the paper to the size wanted (exposing it to as little light as possible) and let the child arrange on it the leaves he wishes to print. He should then place a piece of clear glass on top to keep the design in place. Expose the glass-covered paper to direct sunlight until the

Leaf prints on blueprint paper

background has completely changed color, either to white or very dark, depending on the kind of paper used. After the exposure is complete, the child should then remove it from the sunlight, take off the glass and design leaves, and bathe the paper in the proper solution. Let the print dry and press it flat. These designs are fairly permanent and can be displayed as desired.

Leaf prints on photographic paper

A piece of old sheeting can be used to make an unusual wall hanging. Give your child a small piece of this material and have him paint the entire surface with liquid starch. After the starch has dried, he is ready to draw his design. He can use either undiluted liquid dye, applied with a paintbrush, or permanent felt markers. After the design is completed, the hanging should be pressed. Turn under the side edges and press them flat. To finish the hanging, press under one inch at the top and at the bottom. These folds are made to accommodate the dowels, and the child can then glue them in place.

The colorful batik hangings in the photograph facing page 113 were made using a simplified batik method. Old sheeting provides an

Wall hangings

excellent background. Let the child draw his design on the sheet using crayons. For the color, he will need melted crayons and paraffin. The easiest way to do this is to use small cans or a muffin tin. In each small container, place a piece of paraffin and several pieces of colored crayon, putting a different color in each container. The pans should be set in hot water until the paraffin and crayons have melted. An ideal way to melt the crayons and keep them liquefied is to use an electric frying pan, which keeps the water hot.

Have the child apply the melted crayon with a paintbrush to the sheet following his design. Outlining the design with melted white crayon helps intensify the pattern. Set the design aside and allow it to harden. After the crayon has hardened, he can crumple the sheet—

this produces the cracks which are typical of a batik. The next step in making a batik is dying the fabric.

Dissolve the dye, whether liquid or dry, in hot water using half the amount of water stated in the directions. Allow the dye to cool as hot dye will dissolve the crayon design. Have the child dip the fabric in the dye solution and allow it to set for several minutes. Remove it from the dye and rinse it in cold water. Let the fabric dry until damp. Place the design between pads of newspapers, and let him press it with a warm iron. The heat of the iron dissolves the excess wax and the newspapers act as a blotter.

Although this seems like a complex process, the effort is worthwhile as the child is so delighted with the results of his work. These lovely hangings are especially pretty hung in a sunny window. He is certain to receive many compliments on his unusual wall hangings.

This project, like all of the others in this book, is offered in hopes of bringing your child many hours of enjoyment.

INDEX OF PROJECTS